EVERYONE'S A CRITIC
52 WEEK MOVIE CHALLENGE

FOR FILM BUFFS
AND
CASUAL MOVIE WATCHERS

WATCH, RATE, ANALYZE AND RECORD INFORMATION
ABOUT THE MOVIES YOU WATCH

OTHER TITLES IN THE "CHALLENGE BOOKS" SERIES:

EVERYONE'S A CRITIC - 52 WEEK BOOK CHALLENGE
50 STATE TRAVEL CHALLENGE
EVERYONE'S A FOOD CRITIC - 52 WEEK RESTAURANT CHALLENGE

wandering tortoise

ISBN: 978-1691348138

52 WEEK MOVIE CHALLENGE

COMPLETE THE CHALLENGES IN ANY ORDER.

☑ MOVIE CHALLENGES	COMPLETION DATE
☐ 1. BEST PICTURE WINNER	_____
☐ 2. A MOVIE "CLASSIC"	_____
☐ 3. LOW BUDGET, BIG BOX OFFICE	_____
☐ 4. STARRING ANIMALS	_____
☐ 5. EARLY FILM OF A FAMOUS ACTOR/ACTRESS	_____
☐ 6. WITH SUBTITLES	_____
☐ 7. STOP MOTION FILM	_____
☐ 8. SET DURING AN HISTORIC WAR	_____
☐ 9. INDEPENDENT FILM	_____
☐ 10. FAMILY-FRIENDLY MOVIE	_____
☐ 11. BEST ORIGINAL SCREENPLAY WINNER	_____
☐ 12. CONTROVERSIAL FILM	_____
☐ 13. BASED ON OR TURNED INTO A TV SERIES	_____
☐ 14. BASED ON A TRUE STORY	_____
☐ 15. "B" MOVIE	_____

☑ MOVIE CHALLENGES

- ☐ 16. SILENT FILM
- ☐ 17. ANIMATED FEATURE
- ☐ 18. SET IN THE DISTANT FUTURE
- ☐ 19. RICH VS. POOR
- ☐ 20. SET DURING YOUR FAVORITE TIME PERIOD
- ☐ 21. BEST CINEMATOGRAPHY WINNER
- ☐ 22. MUSICAL
- ☐ 23. SET PRE-1900'S
- ☐ 24. NEW RELEASE
- ☐ 25. 25TH ANNIVERSARY THIS YEAR
- ☐ 26. FEATURES AN ILLNESS
- ☐ 27. STRONG FEMALE LEAD
- ☐ 28. SET DURING THE DECADE YOU WERE BORN
- ☐ 29. BASED AROUND A SPORT
- ☐ 30. A REMAKE
- ☐ 31. FILM FESTIVAL WINNER
- ☐ 32. BLACK & WHITE FILM
- ☐ 33. A SEQUEL
- ☐ 34. SET DURING THE GREAT DEPRESSION

☑ MOVIE CHALLENGES

- [ ] 35. BOOK ADAPTATION
- [ ] 36. YOUR FAVORITE FILM
- [ ] 37. NATURAL DISASTER
- [ ] 38. SET IN YOUR LOCATION OR REGION
- [ ] 39. ABOUT A COMPOSER, MUSICIAN, BAND OR GROUP
- [ ] 40. FOREIGN FILM
- [ ] 41. HOLIDAY MOVIE
- [ ] 42. FIRST FILM OF A FAMOUS DIRECTOR
- [ ] 43. SET IN A COLLEGE
- [ ] 44. BEST MUSIC (ORIGINAL SCORE) WINNER
- [ ] 45. ADAPTED FROM A PLAY
- [ ] 46. WITH YOUR FAVORITE ACTOR/ACTRESS
- [ ] 47. ABOUT A FAMOUS PERSON
- [ ] 48. SET IN A COUNTRY YOU WANT TO VISIT
- [ ] 49. BASED AROUND A RELIGION
- [ ] 50. 50TH ANNIVERSARY THIS YEAR
- [ ] 51. FILM YOU PERSONALLY RELATE TO
- [ ] 52. RELEASED THE DECADE YOU WERE BORN

A FILM THAT HAS WON "BEST PICTURE"

MOVIE TITLE: _____

YEAR RELEASED: _____

ASPECT RATIO: _____ RUN TIME: _____

GENRE: _____ RATED: _____

STARRING: _____

_____

DATE CHALLENGE COMPLETED:

_____

MY RATING:

☆ ☆ ☆ ☆ ☆

DIRECTED BY: _____

PRODUCED BY: _____

WRITTEN BY: _____

MUSIC BY: _____

AWARDS RECEIVED: _____

_____

WHY DID YOU CHOOSE THIS PARTICULAR FILM? _____

_____

HAVE YOU SEEN THIS MOVIE BEFORE? _____

WOULD YOU RECOMMEND THIS FILM? WHY OR WHY NOT? _____

_____

_____

_____

WHICH CHARACTER WERE YOU MOST ABLE TO IDENTIFY WITH OR CONNECT WITH?
IN WHAT WAY? _____

_____

_____

BEST LINE OR MEMORABLE QUOTE: _____

_____

_____

WERE YOU SUPRISED BY THE ENDING? WHAT WOULD YOU DO DIFFERENTLY?

_____

_____

_____

HAVE YOU WATCHED ANY OF THE OTHER "BEST PICTURE" NOMINEES? WHAT
WERE THEY? _____

_____

_____

DO YOU FEEL THIS FILM DESERVED THE AWARD? WHY OR WHY NOT? _____

_____

_____

_____

_____

CHALLENGE #2

A MOVIE "CLASSIC"

MOVIE TITLE: _____

YEAR RELEASED: _____

ASPECT RATIO: _____ RUN TIME: _____

GENRE: _____ RATED: _____

STARRING: _____

_____

DATE CHALLENGE COMPLETED:

_____

MY RATING:

☆ ☆ ☆ ☆ ☆

DIRECTED BY: _____

PRODUCED BY: _____

WRITTEN BY: _____

MUSIC BY: _____

AWARDS RECEIVED: _____

_____

WHY DID YOU CHOOSE THIS PARTICULAR FILM? _____

_____

HAVE YOU SEEN THIS MOVIE BEFORE? _____

WOULD YOU RECOMMEND THIS FILM? WHY OR WHY NOT? _____

_____

_____

_____

WHICH CHARACTER WERE YOU MOST ABLE TO IDENTIFY WITH OR CONNECT WITH? IN WHAT WAY? _____

_____

_____

BEST LINE OR MEMORABLE QUOTE: _____

_____

_____

WERE YOU SUPRISED BY THE ENDING? WHAT WOULD YOU DO DIFFERENTLY?_____

_____

_____

_____

WHAT ELEMENTS OF THIS FILM DO YOU FEEL HAVE HELPED IT BECOME A MOVIE "CLASSIC"?_____

_____

_____

_____

CAN YOU NAME ANY MODERN FILMS THAT HAVE THOSE SAME ELEMENTS?_____

_____

_____

ANYTHING ELSE YOU'D LIKE TO ADD? _____

_____

FILM FACT THE "CASABLANCA" (1942) PREMIERE WAS MOVED TO AN EARLIER DATE TO COINCIDE WITH THE LIBERATION OF CASABLANCA IN WWII

LOW BUDGET, BIG BOX OFFICE

MOVIE TITLE: _____

YEAR RELEASED: _____

ASPECT RATIO: _____ RUN TIME: _____

GENRE: _____ RATED: _____

STARRING: _____

_____

DIRECTED BY: _____

PRODUCED BY: _____

WRITTEN BY: _____

MUSIC BY: _____

AWARDS RECEIVED: _____

_____

WHY DID YOU CHOOSE THIS PARTICULAR FILM? _____

_____

HAVE YOU SEEN THIS MOVIE BEFORE? _____

WOULD YOU RECOMMEND THIS FILM? WHY OR WHY NOT? _____

_____

_____

_____

DATE CHALLENGE COMPLETED:

_____

MY RATING:

☆ ☆ ☆ ☆ ☆

WHICH CHARACTER WERE YOU MOST ABLE TO IDENTIFY WITH OR CONNECT WITH?
IN WHAT WAY? _____

_____

_____

BEST LINE OR MEMORABLE QUOTE: _____

_____

_____

WERE YOU SUPRISED BY THE ENDING? WHAT WOULD YOU DO DIFFERENTLY? _____

_____

_____

_____

DO YOU FEEL A LARGER BUDGET WOULD MAKE THIS FILM BETTER OR WORSE?

_____

HOW WOULD YOU SPEND THE EXTRA FUNDS? _____

_____

_____

_____

_____

_____

ANYTHING ELSE YOU'D LIKE TO ADD? _____

_____

FILM FACT | IN 1976, "ROCKY" COST APPROXIMATELY $1.175 MILLION TO PRODUCE.
ITS BOX OFFICE REVENUE TOTALED $225 MILLION WORLDWIDE!

A FILM
STARRING ANIMALS

MOVIE TITLE: _____

YEAR RELEASED: _____

ASPECT RATIO: _____ RUN TIME: _____

GENRE: _____ RATED: _____

STARRING: _____

_____

DATE CHALLENGE COMPLETED:

_____

MY RATING:

☆ ☆ ☆ ☆ ☆

DIRECTED BY: _____

PRODUCED BY: _____

WRITTEN BY: _____

MUSIC BY: _____

AWARDS RECEIVED: _____

_____

WHY DID YOU CHOOSE THIS PARTICULAR FILM? _____

_____

HAVE YOU SEEN THIS MOVIE BEFORE? _____

WOULD YOU RECOMMEND THIS FILM? WHY OR WHY NOT? _____

_____

_____

_____

WHICH CHARACTER WERE YOU MOST ABLE TO IDENTIFY WITH OR CONNECT WITH?
IN WHAT WAY? _____

_____

_____

BEST LINE OR MEMORABLE QUOTE: _____

_____

_____

WERE YOU SUPRISED BY THE ENDING? WHAT WOULD YOU DO DIFFERENTLY? _____

_____

_____

_____

IF YOU WERE TO MAKE A MOVIE STARRING ANIMALS, WHAT ANIMALS WOULD
CHOOSE? WHY? _____

_____

_____

_____

_____

_____

ANYTHING ELSE YOU'D LIKE TO ADD? _____

_____

THERE WERE 970 ANIMALS ON THE SET OF "BABE" (1995) BUT
ONLY ABOUT 500 OF THEM MADE IT ONTO THE SCREEN.

EARLY FILM OF A
FAMOUS ACTOR/ACTRESS

MOVIE TITLE: _____

YEAR RELEASED: _____

ASPECT RATIO: _____ RUN TIME: _____

GENRE: _____ RATED: _____

STARRING: _____

_____

DATE CHALLENGE COMPLETED:

_____

MY RATING:

☆ ☆ ☆ ☆ ☆

DIRECTED BY: _____

PRODUCED BY: _____

WRITTEN BY: _____

MUSIC BY: _____

AWARDS RECEIVED: _____

_____

WHY DID YOU CHOOSE THIS PARTICULAR FILM? _____

_____

HAVE YOU SEEN THIS MOVIE BEFORE? _____

WOULD YOU RECOMMEND THIS FILM? WHY OR WHY NOT? _____

_____

_____

_____

_____

WHICH CHARACTER WERE YOU MOST ABLE TO IDENTIFY WITH OR CONNECT WITH?
IN WHAT WAY? _____

_____

_____

BEST LINE OR MEMORABLE QUOTE: _____

_____

_____

WERE YOU SUPRISED BY THE ENDING? WHAT WOULD YOU DO DIFFERENTLY? _____

_____

_____

_____

DID YOU SEE HINTS OF THIS STAR'S LATER ACTING STYLE IN THIS EARLY FILM?
IF SO, WHAT WERE THEY? _____

_____

_____

_____

_____

_____

_____

ANYTHING ELSE YOU'D LIKE TO ADD? _____

_____

A FILM
WITH SUBTITLES

MOVIE TITLE: _____

YEAR RELEASED: _____

ASPECT RATIO: _____ RUN TIME: _____

GENRE: _____ RATED: _____

STARRING: _____

_____

DATE CHALLENGE COMPLETED:

_____

MY RATING:

☆ ☆ ☆ ☆ ☆

DIRECTED BY: _____

PRODUCED BY: _____

WRITTEN BY: _____

MUSIC BY: _____

AWARDS RECEIVED: _____

_____

WHY DID YOU CHOOSE THIS PARTICULAR FILM? _____

_____

HAVE YOU SEEN THIS MOVIE BEFORE? _____

WOULD YOU RECOMMEND THIS FILM? WHY OR WHY NOT? _____

_____

_____

_____

WHICH CHARACTER WERE YOU MOST ABLE TO IDENTIFY WITH OR CONNECT WITH? IN WHAT WAY? _____

_____

_____

BEST LINE OR MEMORABLE QUOTE: _____

_____

_____

WERE YOU SUPRISED BY THE ENDING? WHAT WOULD YOU DO DIFFERENTLY?

_____

_____

_____

HOW IMPORTANT IS IT TO YOU TO WATCH A FILM IN ITS NATIVE LANGUAGE?

_____

_____

_____

DO YOU FEEL SUBTITLES LESSEN THE OVERALL MOVIE WATCHING EXPERIENCE?

_____

_____

_____

ANYTHING ELSE YOU'D LIKE TO ADD?_____

_____

ROBERTO BENIGNI (GUIDO) & NICOLETTA BRASCHI (DORA) OF "LIFE IS BEAUTIFUL" (1997) ARE HUSBAND AND WIFE ON SCREEN AND OFF

CHALLENGE #7

A STOP MOTION FILM

MOVIE TITLE: _____

YEAR RELEASED: _____

ASPECT RATIO: _____ RUN TIME: _____

GENRE: _____ RATED: _____

STARRING: _____

DIRECTED BY: _____

PRODUCED BY: _____

WRITTEN BY: _____

MUSIC BY: _____

AWARDS RECEIVED: _____

_____

WHY DID YOU CHOOSE THIS PARTICULAR FILM? _____

_____

HAVE YOU SEEN THIS MOVIE BEFORE? _____

WOULD YOU RECOMMEND THIS FILM? WHY OR WHY NOT? _____

_____

_____

_____

_____

DATE CHALLENGE COMPLETED:

_____

MY RATING:

☆ ☆ ☆ ☆ ☆

WHICH CHARACTER WERE YOU MOST ABLE TO IDENTIFY WITH OR CONNECT WITH?
IN WHAT WAY? _____

_____

_____

BEST LINE OR MEMORABLE QUOTE: _____

_____

_____

WERE YOU SUPRISED BY THE ENDING? WHAT WOULD YOU DO DIFFERENTLY? _____

_____

_____

_____

WHY DO YOU THINK STOP MOTION WAS CHOSEN FOR THIS FILM RATHER THAN
ANIMATION? _____

_____

_____

_____

_____

_____

ANYTHING ELSE YOU'D LIKE TO ADD? _____

_____

FILM FACT IN STOP MOTION, IT TYPICALLY TAKES 12 IMAGES TO CREATE 1 SECOND OF
FILM. THAT EQUALS 64,800 PICTURES NEEDED FOR A 90 MINUTE FILM.

SET DURING
AN HISTORIC WAR

MOVIE TITLE: _____

YEAR RELEASED: _____

ASPECT RATIO: _____ RUN TIME: _____

GENRE: _____ RATED: _____

STARRING: _____

_____

DIRECTED BY: _____

PRODUCED BY: _____

WRITTEN BY: _____

MUSIC BY: _____

AWARDS RECEIVED: _____

_____

WHY DID YOU CHOOSE THIS PARTICULAR FILM? _____

_____

HAVE YOU SEEN THIS MOVIE BEFORE? _____

WOULD YOU RECOMMEND THIS FILM? WHY OR WHY NOT? _____

_____

_____

_____

DATE CHALLENGE COMPLETED:

_____

MY RATING:

☆ ☆ ☆ ☆ ☆

WHICH CHARACTER WERE YOU MOST ABLE TO IDENTIFY WITH OR CONNECT WITH? IN WHAT WAY? _____

_____

_____

BEST LINE OR MEMORABLE QUOTE: _____

_____

_____

WERE YOU SUPRISED BY THE ENDING? WHAT WOULD YOU DO DIFFERENTLY?_____

_____

_____

_____

IN WHAT WAYS DO YOU FEEL THE FILM DID OR DID NOT PORTRAY THE TIME PERIOD ACCURATELY?_____

_____

_____

_____

_____

_____

_____

ANYTHING ELSE YOU'D LIKE TO ADD?_____

_____

GEORGE C. SCOTT REFUSED HIS ACADEMY AWARD FOR "PATTON" (1970). HE WAS THE FIRST PERSON TO EVER DO SO.

AN
INDEPENDENT FILM

MOVIE TITLE: _____

YEAR RELEASED: _____

ASPECT RATIO: _____ RUN TIME: _____

GENRE: _____ RATED: _____

STARRING: _____

_____

DATE CHALLENGE COMPLETED:

_____

MY RATING:

☆ ☆ ☆ ☆ ☆

DIRECTED BY: _____

PRODUCED BY: _____

WRITTEN BY: _____

MUSIC BY: _____

AWARDS RECEIVED: _____

_____

WHY DID YOU CHOOSE THIS PARTICULAR FILM? _____

_____

HAVE YOU SEEN THIS MOVIE BEFORE? _____

WOULD YOU RECOMMEND THIS FILM? WHY OR WHY NOT? _____

_____

_____

_____

WHICH CHARACTER WERE YOU MOST ABLE TO IDENTIFY WITH OR CONNECT WITH?
IN WHAT WAY? _____

_____

_____

BEST LINE OR MEMORABLE QUOTE: _____

_____

_____

WERE YOU SUPRISED BY THE ENDING? WHAT WOULD YOU DO DIFFERENTLY?_____

_____

_____

_____

DO YOU USUALLY PREFER TO WATCH INDIE FILMS OVER HOLLYWOOD BIG STUDIO
PRODUCTIONS? WHY OR WHY NOT?_____

_____

_____

_____

_____

_____

_____

ANYTHING ELSE YOU'D LIKE TO ADD?_____

_____

A FAMILY-FRIENDLY MOVIE

MOVIE TITLE: _____

YEAR RELEASED: _____

ASPECT RATIO: _____ RUN TIME: _____

GENRE: _____ RATED: _____

STARRING: _____

_____

DIRECTED BY: _____

PRODUCED BY: _____

WRITTEN BY: _____

MUSIC BY: _____

AWARDS RECEIVED: _____

_____

DATE CHALLENGE COMPLETED:

_____

MY RATING:

☆ ☆ ☆ ☆ ☆

WHY DID YOU CHOOSE THIS PARTICULAR FILM? _____

_____

HAVE YOU SEEN THIS MOVIE BEFORE? _____

WOULD YOU RECOMMEND THIS FILM? WHY OR WHY NOT? _____

_____

_____

_____

WHICH CHARACTER WERE YOU MOST ABLE TO IDENTIFY WITH OR CONNECT WITH?
IN WHAT WAY? _____

_____

_____

BEST LINE OR MEMORABLE QUOTE: _____

_____

_____

WERE YOU SUPRISED BY THE ENDING? WHAT WOULD YOU DO DIFFERENTLY?_____

_____

_____

_____

WHAT ELEMENTS DO YOU BELEIVE ARE NECESSARY TO CREATE AN ENTERTAINING
FAMILY-ORIENTED FILM? DO YOU FEEL THIS MOVIE HAD THOSE THINGS?_____

_____

_____

_____

_____

_____

_____

ANYTHING ELSE YOU'D LIKE TO ADD?_____

_____

A FILM THAT HAS WON
BEST ORIGINAL SCREENPLAY

MOVIE TITLE: _____

YEAR RELEASED: _____

ASPECT RATIO: _____ RUN TIME: _____

GENRE: _____ RATED: _____

STARRING: _____

_____

DATE CHALLENGE COMPLETED:

_____

MY RATING:

☆ ☆ ☆ ☆ ☆

DIRECTED BY: _____

PRODUCED BY: _____

WRITTEN BY: _____

MUSIC BY: _____

AWARDS RECEIVED: _____

_____

WHY DID YOU CHOOSE THIS PARTICULAR FILM? _____

_____

HAVE YOU SEEN THIS MOVIE BEFORE? _____

WOULD YOU RECOMMEND THIS FILM? WHY OR WHY NOT? _____

_____

_____

_____

WHICH CHARACTER WERE YOU MOST ABLE TO IDENTIFY WITH OR CONNECT WITH?
IN WHAT WAY? _____

_____

_____

BEST LINE OR MEMORABLE QUOTE: _____

_____

_____

WERE YOU SUPRISED BY THE ENDING? WHAT WOULD YOU DO DIFFERENTLY? ____

_____

_____

_____

UNLESS YOU READ THE SCRIPT, YOU CAN ONLY JUDGE A SCREENPLAY BY THE
MOVIE. BASED ON THE MOVIE, DO YOU FEEL THIS SCRIPT DESERVED THE AWARD
FOR BEST SCREENPLAY? EXPLAIN. _____

_____

_____

_____

_____

_____

ANYTHING ELSE YOU'D LIKE TO ADD? _____

_____

SNOW IS EXPENSIVE TO REPLICATE SO FILMING OF "DEAD POETS
SOCIETY" (1989) WAS MOVED FROM GEORGIA TO DELAWARE.

A CONTROVERSIAL FILM

MOVIE TITLE: _____

YEAR RELEASED: _____

ASPECT RATIO: _____ RUN TIME: _____

GENRE: _____ RATED: _____

STARRING: _____

_____

DIRECTED BY: _____

PRODUCED BY: _____

WRITTEN BY: _____

MUSIC BY: _____

AWARDS RECEIVED: _____

_____

DATE CHALLENGE COMPLETED:

_____

MY RATING:

☆☆☆☆☆

WHY DID YOU CHOOSE THIS PARTICULAR FILM? _____

_____

HAVE YOU SEEN THIS MOVIE BEFORE? _____

WOULD YOU RECOMMEND THIS FILM? WHY OR WHY NOT? _____

_____

_____

_____

WHICH CHARACTER WERE YOU MOST ABLE TO IDENTIFY WITH OR CONNECT WITH? IN WHAT WAY? _____

_____

_____

BEST LINE OR MEMORABLE QUOTE: _____

_____

_____

WERE YOU SUPRISED BY THE ENDING? WHAT WOULD YOU DO DIFFERENTLY? _____

_____

_____

_____

WHAT IS/WAS THE CONTROVERSY SURROUNDING THIS FILM? _____

_____

_____

_____

AFTER WATCHING THE FILM, CAN YOU SEE BOTH SIDES OF THE ARGUEMENT? _____

_____

_____

_____

ANYTHING ELSE YOU'D LIKE TO ADD? _____

_____

THE STUDIO, EXPECTING "BONNIE AND CLYDE" (1967) TO FLOP, PAID WARREN BEATTY 40% OF GROSS. BEATTY MADE MILLIONS.

BASED ON A TELEVISION SERIES OR TURNED INTO A TELEVISION SERIES

MOVIE TITLE: _____

YEAR RELEASED: _____

ASPECT RATIO: _____ RUN TIME: _____

GENRE: _____ RATED: _____

STARRING: _____

_____

DATE CHALLENGE COMPLETED:

_____

MY RATING:

☆ ☆ ☆ ☆ ☆

DIRECTED BY: _____

PRODUCED BY: _____

WRITTEN BY: _____

MUSIC BY: _____

AWARDS RECEIVED: _____

_____

WHY DID YOU CHOOSE THIS PARTICULAR FILM? _____

_____

HAVE YOU SEEN THIS MOVIE BEFORE? _____

WOULD YOU RECOMMEND THIS FILM? WHY OR WHY NOT? _____

_____

_____

_____

WHICH CHARACTER WERE YOU MOST ABLE TO IDENTIFY WITH OR CONNECT WITH?
IN WHAT WAY? _____
_____
_____

BEST LINE OR MEMORABLE QUOTE: _____
_____
_____

WERE YOU SUPRISED BY THE ENDING? WHAT WOULD YOU DO DIFFERENTLY? _____
_____
_____

IF YOU HAVE SEEN THE TELEVISION SERIES, DO YOU PREFER THE MOVIE OR THE
TV VERSION? WHY? _____
_____
_____
_____
_____
_____

ANYTHING ELSE YOU'D LIKE TO ADD? _____
_____

BASED ON
A TRUE STORY

MOVIE TITLE: _____

YEAR RELEASED: _____

| DATE CHALLENGE COMPLETED: |

ASPECT RATIO: _____ RUN TIME: _____

| _____ |

GENRE: _____ RATED: _____

| MY RATING: |

STARRING: _____

☆ ☆ ☆ ☆ ☆

_____

DIRECTED BY: _____

PRODUCED BY: _____

WRITTEN BY: _____

MUSIC BY: _____

AWARDS RECEIVED: _____

_____

WHY DID YOU CHOOSE THIS PARTICULAR FILM? _____

_____

HAVE YOU SEEN THIS MOVIE BEFORE? _____

WOULD YOU RECOMMEND THIS FILM? WHY OR WHY NOT? _____

_____

_____

_____

WHICH CHARACTER WERE YOU MOST ABLE TO IDENTIFY WITH OR CONNECT WITH?
IN WHAT WAY? _____

_____

_____

BEST LINE OR MEMORABLE QUOTE: _____

_____

_____

WERE YOU SUPRISED BY THE ENDING? WHAT WOULD YOU DO DIFFERENTLY?_____

_____

_____

AFTER WATCHING THIS FILM, DID YOU WANT TO LEARN MORE ABOUT THE TRUE
STORY? WHY OR WHY NOT?_____

_____

_____

_____

_____

_____

_____

ANYTHING ELSE YOU'D LIKE TO ADD?_____

_____

FILM FACT 250 HOMELESS PEOPLE WERE HIRED FOR TWO DAYS TO PLAY
THEMSELVES IN "THE PURSUIT OF HAPPYNESS" (2006).

A "B" MOVIE

MOVIE TITLE: _____

YEAR RELEASED: _____

ASPECT RATIO: _____ RUN TIME: _____

GENRE: _____ RATED: _____

STARRING: _____

_____

DIRECTED BY: _____

PRODUCED BY: _____

WRITTEN BY: _____

MUSIC BY: _____

AWARDS RECEIVED: _____

_____

WHY DID YOU CHOOSE THIS PARTICULAR FILM? _____

_____

HAVE YOU SEEN THIS MOVIE BEFORE? _____

WOULD YOU RECOMMEND THIS FILM? WHY OR WHY NOT? _____

_____

_____

_____

DATE CHALLENGE COMPLETED:

_____

MY RATING:

☆☆☆☆☆

WHICH CHARACTER WERE YOU MOST ABLE TO IDENTIFY WITH OR CONNECT WITH?
IN WHAT WAY? _____

_____

_____

BEST LINE OR MEMORABLE QUOTE: _____

_____

_____

WERE YOU SUPRISED BY THE ENDING? WHAT WOULD YOU DO DIFFERENTLY? _____

_____

_____

_____

_____

WHAT CHANGES WOULD YOU IMPLEMENT TO MAKE THIS AN "A LIST" MOVIE?

_____

_____

_____

_____

_____

_____

ANYTHING ELSE YOU'D LIKE TO ADD? _____

_____

IT IS ESTIMATED THAT HALF OF THE FILMS PRODUCED BY THE
FILM FACT EIGHT MAJOR STUDIOS DURING THE 1930'S WERE "B" MOVIES.

CHOOSE A
SILENT FILM

MOVIE TITLE: _____

YEAR RELEASED: _____

ASPECT RATIO: _____ RUN TIME: _____

GENRE: _____ RATED: _____

STARRING: _____
_____

DATE CHALLENGE COMPLETED:

_____

MY RATING:

☆ ☆ ☆ ☆ ☆

DIRECTED BY: _____

PRODUCED BY: _____

WRITTEN BY: _____

MUSIC BY: _____

AWARDS RECEIVED: _____
_____

WHY DID YOU CHOOSE THIS PARTICULAR FILM? _____
_____

HAVE YOU SEEN THIS MOVIE BEFORE? _____

WOULD YOU RECOMMEND THIS FILM? WHY OR WHY NOT? _____
_____
_____
_____

WHICH CHARACTER WERE YOU MOST ABLE TO IDENTIFY WITH OR CONNECT WITH?
IN WHAT WAY? _____

_____

_____

BEST LINE OR MEMORABLE QUOTE: _____

_____

_____

WERE YOU SUPRISED BY THE ENDING? WHAT WOULD YOU DO DIFFERENTLY?_____

_____

_____

_____

WITH THE MUSIC, THE ACTOR'S BODY LANGUAGE, AND THE TITLE CARDS HELPING
TO TELL THE STORY, WERE YOU ABLE TO FOLLOW ALONG?_____

_____

WOULD YOU LIKE TO SEE MORE SILENT FILMS MADE TODAY? WHY OR WHY NOT?

_____

_____

_____

_____

ANYTHING ELSE YOU'D LIKE TO ADD?_____

_____

A BATTLE SCENE IN "THE GENERAL" (1926) SPARKED A FOREST FIRE.
PRODUCTION STOPPED SO THE FILM CREW COULD FIGHT THE FIRE.

AN
ANIMATED FEATURE FILM

MOVIE TITLE: _____

YEAR RELEASED: _____

ASPECT RATIO: _____ RUN TIME: _____

GENRE: _____ RATED: _____

STARRING: _____

_____

DATE CHALLENGE COMPLETED:

_____

MY RATING:

☆ ☆ ☆ ☆ ☆

DIRECTED BY: _____

PRODUCED BY: _____

WRITTEN BY: _____

MUSIC BY: _____

AWARDS RECEIVED: _____

_____

WHY DID YOU CHOOSE THIS PARTICULAR FILM? _____

_____

HAVE YOU SEEN THIS MOVIE BEFORE? _____

WOULD YOU RECOMMEND THIS FILM? WHY OR WHY NOT? _____

_____

_____

_____

WHICH CHARACTER WERE YOU MOST ABLE TO IDENTIFY WITH OR CONNECT WITH?
IN WHAT WAY? _____

_____

_____

BEST LINE OR MEMORABLE QUOTE: _____

_____

_____

WERE YOU SUPRISED BY THE ENDING? WHAT WOULD YOU DO DIFFERENTLY?

_____

_____

_____

WHO WOULD YOU WANT TO SEE STAR IN A LIVE ACTION VERSION OF THIS
FILM? WHY? _____

_____

_____

_____

_____

_____

ANYTHING ELSE YOU'D LIKE TO ADD? _____

_____

 IN 2001, "SHREK" WAS THE FIRST ANIMATED FILM TO WIN THE NEW
FILM FACT "BEST ANIMATED FEATURE" OSCAR.

CHALLENGE #18

SET IN THE
DISTANT FUTURE

MOVIE TITLE: _____

YEAR RELEASED: _____

ASPECT RATIO: _____ RUN TIME: _____

GENRE: _____ RATED: _____

STARRING: _____

_____

DATE CHALLENGE COMPLETED:

_____

MY RATING:

☆ ☆ ☆ ☆ ☆

DIRECTED BY: _____

PRODUCED BY: _____

WRITTEN BY: _____

MUSIC BY: _____

AWARDS RECEIVED: _____

_____

WHY DID YOU CHOOSE THIS PARTICULAR FILM? _____

_____

HAVE YOU SEEN THIS MOVIE BEFORE? _____

WOULD YOU RECOMMEND THIS FILM? WHY OR WHY NOT? _____

_____

_____

_____

WHICH CHARACTER WERE YOU MOST ABLE TO IDENTIFY WITH OR CONNECT WITH? IN WHAT WAY? _____

_____

_____

BEST LINE OR MEMORABLE QUOTE: _____

_____

_____

WERE YOU SUPRISED BY THE ENDING? WHAT WOULD YOU DO DIFFERENTLY? _____

_____

_____

_____

IMAGINE LIFE AS PORTRAYED IN THIS FILM BECOMING A REALITY. TELL WHY THIS SCENARIO IS OR ISN'T DESIREABLE. _____

_____

_____

_____

_____

_____

_____

ANYTHING ELSE YOU'D LIKE TO ADD? _____

_____

 MADE IN 1902, "LE VOYAGE DANS LA LUNE" BY GEORGE MÉLIÈS (A TRIP TO THE MOON) IS THOUGHT TO BE THE FIRST SCIENCE FICTION FILM.

RICH VS. POOR

MOVIE TITLE: _____

YEAR RELEASED: _____

ASPECT RATIO: _____ RUN TIME: _____

GENRE: _____ RATED: _____

STARRING: _____

_____

DATE CHALLENGE COMPLETED:

_____

MY RATING:

☆ ☆ ☆ ☆ ☆

DIRECTED BY: _____

PRODUCED BY: _____

WRITTEN BY: _____

MUSIC BY: _____

AWARDS RECEIVED: _____

_____

WHY DID YOU CHOOSE THIS PARTICULAR FILM?_____

_____

HAVE YOU SEEN THIS MOVIE BEFORE?_____

WOULD YOU RECOMMEND THIS FILM? WHY OR WHY NOT?_____

_____

_____

_____

WHICH CHARACTER WERE YOU MOST ABLE TO IDENTIFY WITH OR CONNECT WITH?
IN WHAT WAY? _____

_____

_____

BEST LINE OR MEMORABLE QUOTE: _____

_____

_____

WERE YOU SUPRISED BY THE ENDING? WHAT WOULD YOU DO DIFFERENTLY? _____

_____

_____

_____

HOW DO YOU FEEL THE CLASS OR INCOME DISPARITY CONTRIBUTES TO THE
CONFLICT OF THE STORY? _____

_____

_____

_____

_____

_____

ANYTHING ELSE YOU'D LIKE TO ADD? _____

_____

FILM FACT "TRADING PLACES" (1983) INSPIRED A NEW RULE ON WALL STREET BARRING
PEOPLE FROM USING SECRET INSIDE INFORMATION TO CORNER MARKETS

SET DURING YOUR
FAVORITE TIME PERIOD

MOVIE TITLE: _____

YEAR RELEASED: _____

ASPECT RATIO: _____ RUN TIME: _____

GENRE: _____ RATED: _____

STARRING: _____

_____

DIRECTED BY: _____

PRODUCED BY: _____

WRITTEN BY: _____

MUSIC BY: _____

AWARDS RECEIVED: _____

_____

WHY DID YOU CHOOSE THIS PARTICULAR FILM? _____

_____

HAVE YOU SEEN THIS MOVIE BEFORE? _____

WOULD YOU RECOMMEND THIS FILM? WHY OR WHY NOT? _____

_____

_____

_____

| DATE CHALLENGE COMPLETED: |
| _____ |
| MY RATING: |
| ☆ ☆ ☆ ☆ ☆ |

WHICH CHARACTER WERE YOU MOST ABLE TO IDENTIFY WITH OR CONNECT WITH?
IN WHAT WAY? _____
_____
_____

BEST LINE OR MEMORABLE QUOTE: _____
_____
_____

WERE YOU SUPRISED BY THE ENDING? WHAT WOULD YOU DO DIFFERENTLY? _____
_____
_____
_____

WHY IS THIS YOUR FAVORITE TIME PERIOD? _____
_____
_____
_____

HOW WELL DID THE FILM CAPTURE THE "FEEL" OF THE TIME PERIOD? EXPLAIN.
_____
_____
_____

ANYTHING ELSE YOU'D LIKE TO ADD? _____
_____

FILM FACT "THE STORY OF THE KELLY GANG" (1906) WAS THE FIRST FEATURE-
LENGTH MOVIE. IT WAS FILMED IN MELBOURNE, AUSTRALIA.

A FILM THAT HAS WON
BEST CINEMATOGRAPHY

MOVIE TITLE: _____

YEAR RELEASED:_____

ASPECT RATIO: _____ RUN TIME: _____

GENRE: _____ RATED: _____

STARRING: _____
_____

DIRECTED BY: _____

PRODUCED BY: _____

WRITTEN BY: _____

MUSIC BY: _____

AWARDS RECEIVED: _____
_____

WHY DID YOU CHOOSE THIS PARTICULAR FILM?_____
_____

HAVE YOU SEEN THIS MOVIE BEFORE?_____

WOULD YOU RECOMMEND THIS FILM? WHY OR WHY NOT?_____
_____
_____
_____

DATE CHALLENGE COMPLETED:

_____

MY RATING:

☆ ☆ ☆ ☆ ☆

WHICH CHARACTER WERE YOU MOST ABLE TO IDENTIFY WITH OR CONNECT WITH?
IN WHAT WAY? _____

_____

_____

BEST LINE OR MEMORABLE QUOTE: _____

_____

_____

WERE YOU SUPRISED BY THE ENDING? WHAT WOULD YOU DO DIFFERENTLY? ____

_____

_____

_____

DO YOU FEEL THE CINEMATOGRAPHY IN THIS FILM ENHANCED IT OR CARRIED IT?
IN WHAT WAYS? _____

_____

_____

_____

_____

_____

ANYTHING ELSE YOU'D LIKE TO ADD? _____

_____

 DOROTHY WAS SUPPOSED TO HAVE SILVER SLIPPERS IN "THE WIZARD OF
FILM FACT OZ" (1939) BUT THE RUBY SLIPPERS SHOWED UP BETTER ON FILM.

A MUSICAL

MOVIE TITLE: _____

YEAR RELEASED:_____

ASPECT RATIO: _____ RUN TIME: _____

GENRE: _____ RATED:_____

STARRING: _____

_____

DATE CHALLENGE COMPLETED:

_____

MY RATING:

☆☆☆☆☆

DIRECTED BY: _____

PRODUCED BY: _____

WRITTEN BY: _____

MUSIC BY: _____

AWARDS RECEIVED: _____

_____

WHY DID YOU CHOOSE THIS PARTICULAR FILM?_____

_____

HAVE YOU SEEN THIS MOVIE BEFORE?_____

WOULD YOU RECOMMEND THIS FILM? WHY OR WHY NOT?_____

_____

_____

_____

WHICH CHARACTER WERE YOU MOST ABLE TO IDENTIFY WITH OR CONNECT WITH?
IN WHAT WAY? _____

_____

_____

BEST LINE OR MEMORABLE QUOTE: _____

_____

_____

WERE YOU SUPRISED BY THE ENDING? WHAT WOULD YOU DO DIFFERENTLY? _____

_____

_____

_____

DO YOU NORMALLY ENJOY MUSICALS? _____
DO YOU FEEL THE FILM WAS ENHANCED BY THE MUSICAL NUMBERS? WHY OR
WHY NOT? _____

_____

_____

_____

_____

_____

ANYTHING ELSE YOU'D LIKE TO ADD? _____

_____

FILM FACT "THE SOUND OF MUSIC" (1959) WAS THE LAST OF THE RODGERS AND
HAMMERSTEIN MUSICALS. HAMMERSTEIN DIED IN 1960.

A FILM THAT TAKES PLACE
BEFORE THE YEAR 1900

MOVIE TITLE: _____

YEAR RELEASED: _____

ASPECT RATIO: _____ RUN TIME: _____

GENRE: _____ RATED: _____

STARRING: _____

_____

DATE CHALLENGE COMPLETED:

_____

MY RATING:

☆☆☆☆☆

DIRECTED BY: _____

PRODUCED BY: _____

WRITTEN BY: _____

MUSIC BY: _____

AWARDS RECEIVED: _____

_____

WHY DID YOU CHOOSE THIS PARTICULAR FILM? _____

_____

HAVE YOU SEEN THIS MOVIE BEFORE? _____

WOULD YOU RECOMMEND THIS FILM? WHY OR WHY NOT? _____

_____

_____

_____

_____

WHICH CHARACTER WERE YOU MOST ABLE TO IDENTIFY WITH OR CONNECT WITH?
IN WHAT WAY? _____

_____

_____

BEST LINE OR MEMORABLE QUOTE: _____

_____

_____

WERE YOU SUPRISED BY THE ENDING? WHAT WOULD YOU DO DIFFERENTLY? ____

_____

_____

_____

IMAGINE YOURSELF LIVING IN THIS TIME PERIOD IN THE SAME PLACE YOUR FILM
WAS SET. WHAT THINGS WOULD YOU BE EXCITED TO WITNESS OR EXPERIENCE?

_____

_____

_____

_____

_____

ANYTHING ELSE YOU'D LIKE TO ADD? _____

_____

 "CAPTAIN BLOOD" (1935) WAS THE FIRST OF NINE FILMS STARRING
OLIVIA DE HAVILLAND AND ERROL FLYNN TOGETHER

CHALLENGE #24

A NEW RELEASE

MOVIE TITLE: _____

YEAR RELEASED: _____

ASPECT RATIO: _____ RUN TIME: _____

GENRE: _____ RATED: _____

STARRING: _____

_____

DIRECTED BY: _____

PRODUCED BY: _____

WRITTEN BY: _____

MUSIC BY: _____

AWARDS RECEIVED: _____

_____

WHY DID YOU CHOOSE THIS PARTICULAR FILM? _____

_____

HAVE YOU SEEN THIS MOVIE BEFORE? _____

WOULD YOU RECOMMEND THIS FILM? WHY OR WHY NOT? _____

_____

_____

_____

DATE CHALLENGE COMPLETED:

_____

MY RATING:

☆☆☆☆☆

WHICH CHARACTER WERE YOU MOST ABLE TO IDENTIFY WITH OR CONNECT WITH? IN WHAT WAY? _____

_____

_____

BEST LINE OR MEMORABLE QUOTE: _____

_____

_____

WERE YOU SUPRISED BY THE ENDING? WHAT WOULD YOU DO DIFFERENTLY? _____

_____

_____

_____

BASED ON PRE-RELEASE MARKETING, AND WORD OF MOUTH, WHAT EXPECTATIONS DID YOU HAVE OF THIS MOVIE? _____

_____

_____

_____

DID THIS FILM MEET YOUR EXPECTATIONS? WHY OR WHY NOT? _____

_____

_____

_____

_____

 THE AVERAGE MOVIE TICKET PRICE IN THE U.S. 1948 WAS 36 CENTS. BY 2019, THE AVERAGE PRICE HAD RISEN TO $9.01 PER TICKET!

A FILM CELEBRATING ITS
25TH ANNIVERSARY THIS YEAR

MOVIE TITLE: _____

YEAR RELEASED: _____

ASPECT RATIO: _____ RUN TIME: _____

GENRE: _____ RATED: _____

STARRING: _____

_____

DATE CHALLENGE COMPLETED:

_____

MY RATING:

☆ ☆ ☆ ☆ ☆

DIRECTED BY: _____

PRODUCED BY: _____

WRITTEN BY: _____

MUSIC BY: _____

AWARDS RECEIVED: _____

_____

WHY DID YOU CHOOSE THIS PARTICULAR FILM? _____

_____

HAVE YOU SEEN THIS MOVIE BEFORE? _____

WOULD YOU RECOMMEND THIS FILM? WHY OR WHY NOT? ___

_____

_____

_____

WHICH CHARACTER WERE YOU MOST ABLE TO IDENTIFY WITH OR CONNECT WITH?
IN WHAT WAY? _____

_____

_____

BEST LINE OR MEMORABLE QUOTE: _____

_____

_____

WERE YOU SUPRISED BY THE ENDING? WHAT WOULD YOU DO DIFFERENTLY? _____

_____

_____

_____

DO YOU FEEL THIS FILM SHOWS AS WELL AS IT DID WHEN IT WAS RELEASED 25
YEARS AGO? EXPLAIN. _____

_____

_____

_____

_____

_____

ANYTHING ELSE YOU'D LIKE TO ADD? _____

_____

IN 2019, "PULP FICTION", "FORREST GUMP" AND "THE LION KING"
ALL CELEBRATED THEIR 25TH ANNIVERSARIES

A FILM THAT
FEATURES AN ILLNESS

MOVIE TITLE: _____

YEAR RELEASED: _____

ASPECT RATIO: _____ RUN TIME: _____

GENRE: _____ RATED: _____

STARRING: _____

_____

DATE CHALLENGE COMPLETED:

_____

MY RATING:

☆ ☆ ☆ ☆ ☆

DIRECTED BY: _____

PRODUCED BY: _____

WRITTEN BY: _____

MUSIC BY: _____

AWARDS RECEIVED: _____

_____

WHY DID YOU CHOOSE THIS PARTICULAR FILM? _____

_____

HAVE YOU SEEN THIS MOVIE BEFORE? _____

WOULD YOU RECOMMEND THIS FILM? WHY OR WHY NOT? _____

_____

_____

_____

WHICH CHARACTER WERE YOU MOST ABLE TO IDENTIFY WITH OR CONNECT WITH? IN WHAT WAY? _____

_____

_____

BEST LINE OR MEMORABLE QUOTE: _____

_____

WERE YOU SUPRISED BY THE ENDING? WHAT WOULD YOU DO DIFFERENTLY?

_____

_____

_____

WHAT IS THE ILLNESS FEATURED IN THE FILM?_____

IS THE ILLNESS ONE YOU WERE PREVIOUSLY AWARE OF OR FAMILIAR WITH? IF SO, HOW?_____

_____

_____

AFTER SEEING THIS FILM, HOW DO YOU THINK YOU WILL INTERACT WITH SOME- ONE WHO HAS THIS ILLNESS?_____

_____

_____

ANYTHING ELSE YOU'D LIKE TO ADD?_____

_____

FILM FACT "WIND BENEATH MY WINGS" WAS ALMOST CUT FROM THE SOUND- TRACK FOR "BEACHES" (1989). IT WON TWO GRAMMY AWARDS.

A FILM WITH
A STRONG FEMALE LEAD

MOVIE TITLE: _____

YEAR RELEASED: _____

ASPECT RATIO: _____ RUN TIME: _____

GENRE: _____ RATED: _____

STARRING: _____

_____

DIRECTED BY: _____

PRODUCED BY: _____

WRITTEN BY: _____

MUSIC BY: _____

AWARDS RECEIVED: _____

_____

WHY DID YOU CHOOSE THIS PARTICULAR FILM? _____

_____

HAVE YOU SEEN THIS MOVIE BEFORE? _____

WOULD YOU RECOMMEND THIS FILM? WHY OR WHY NOT? _____

_____

_____

_____

DATE CHALLENGE COMPLETED:

_____

MY RATING:

☆ ☆ ☆ ☆ ☆

WHICH CHARACTER WERE YOU MOST ABLE TO IDENTIFY WITH OR CONNECT WITH? IN WHAT WAY? _____

_____

_____

BEST LINE OR MEMORABLE QUOTE: _____

_____

_____

WERE YOU SUPRISED BY THE ENDING? WHAT WOULD YOU DO DIFFERENTLY? _____

_____

_____

_____

WHAT ATTRIBUTES DOES THE MAIN CHARACTER BRING TO HER ROLE?

_____

_____

_____

DO THOSE FEATURES HELP THE AUDIENCE TO CONNECT WITH BOTH HER AND HER STORY? IF SO, HOW? _____

_____

_____

ANYTHING ELSE YOU'D LIKE TO ADD? _____

_____

 WHEN JULIA ROBERTS MADE "ERIN BROCKOVICH" (2000), SHE BECAME
FILM FACT THE FIRST FEMALE TO EARN $20 MILLION FOR A MOVIE.

SET DURING
THE DECADE YOU WERE BORN

MOVIE TITLE: _____

YEAR RELEASED: _____

ASPECT RATIO: _____ RUN TIME: _____

GENRE: _____ RATED: _____

STARRING: _____

_____

DATE CHALLENGE COMPLETED:

_____

MY RATING:

☆ ☆ ☆ ☆ ☆

DIRECTED BY: _____

PRODUCED BY: _____

WRITTEN BY: _____

MUSIC BY: _____

AWARDS RECEIVED: _____

_____

WHY DID YOU CHOOSE THIS PARTICULAR FILM? _____

_____

HAVE YOU SEEN THIS MOVIE BEFORE? _____

WOULD YOU RECOMMEND THIS FILM? WHY OR WHY NOT? _____

_____

_____

_____

WHICH CHARACTER WERE YOU MOST ABLE TO IDENTIFY WITH OR CONNECT WITH? IN WHAT WAY? _____

_____

_____

BEST LINE OR MEMORABLE QUOTE: _____

_____

_____

WERE YOU SUPRISED BY THE ENDING? WHAT WOULD YOU DO DIFFERENTLY? _____

_____

_____

HOW WELL DID THE FILM CAPTURE THE "FEEL" OF THE TIME PERIOD? EXPLAIN.

_____

_____

_____

_____

_____

_____

ANYTHING ELSE YOU'D LIKE TO ADD? _____

_____

FILM FACT OVER 3000 STATUETTES HAVE BEEN AWARDED SINCE THE INCEPTION OF THE ACADEMY AWARDS CEREMONY IN 1929

BASED AROUND
A SPORT

MOVIE TITLE: _____

YEAR RELEASED: _____

ASPECT RATIO: _____ RUN TIME: _____

GENRE: _____ RATED: _____

STARRING: _____

_____

DATE CHALLENGE COMPLETED:

_____

MY RATING:

☆☆☆☆☆

DIRECTED BY: _____

PRODUCED BY: _____

WRITTEN BY: _____

MUSIC BY: _____

AWARDS RECEIVED: _____

_____

WHY DID YOU CHOOSE THIS PARTICULAR FILM? _____

_____

HAVE YOU SEEN THIS MOVIE BEFORE? _____

WOULD YOU RECOMMEND THIS FILM? WHY OR WHY NOT? _____

_____

_____

_____

WHICH CHARACTER WERE YOU MOST ABLE TO IDENTIFY WITH OR CONNECT WITH? IN WHAT WAY? _____

_____

_____

BEST LINE OR MEMORABLE QUOTE: _____

_____

_____

WERE YOU SUPRISED BY THE ENDING? WHAT WOULD YOU DO DIFFERENTLY? _____

_____

_____

_____

ARE YOU FAMILIAR WITH THIS SPORT? IF SO, HOW? _____

_____

_____

DO YOU HAVE A NEW APPRECIATION FOR THE SPORT AND THOSE WHO CHOOSE TO PARTICIPATE IN IT? WHY OR WHY NOT? _____

_____

_____

_____

ANYTHING ELSE YOU'D LIKE TO ADD? _____

_____

 FOR THE FINAL FIGHT IN "CINDERELLA MAN" (2005) THE ARENA
FILM FACT WAS FILLED WITH 1000 EXTRAS AND 15,000 INFLATABLE DOLLS

A REMAKE

MOVIE TITLE: _____

YEAR RELEASED:_____

ASPECT RATIO:_____ RUN TIME: _____

GENRE: _____ RATED:_____

STARRING: _____

_____

DATE CHALLENGE COMPLETED:

_____

MY RATING:

☆ ☆ ☆ ☆ ☆

DIRECTED BY: _____

PRODUCED BY: _____

WRITTEN BY: _____

MUSIC BY:_____

AWARDS RECEIVED: _____

_____

WHY DID YOU CHOOSE THIS PARTICULAR FILM?_____

_____

HAVE YOU SEEN THIS MOVIE BEFORE?_____

WOULD YOU RECOMMEND THIS FILM? WHY OR WHY NOT?_____

_____

_____

_____

WHICH CHARACTER WERE YOU MOST ABLE TO IDENTIFY WITH OR CONNECT WITH?
IN WHAT WAY? _____

_____

_____

BEST LINE OR MEMORABLE QUOTE: _____

_____

_____

DO YOU FEEL THIS FILM WAS BETTER OR WORSE THAN THE ORIGINAL? WHY? ____

_____

_____

_____

DID THE FILM FOLLOW THE ORIGINAL STORYLINE, OR DID IT CREATE SOMETHING
NEW? _____

_____

_____

IS THERE ANYTHING YOU WOULD HAVE DONE DIFFERENTLY? _____

_____

_____

_____

ANYTHING ELSE YOU'D LIKE TO ADD? _____

_____

FILM FACT "A STAR IS BORN" HAS HAD SEVERAL INCARNATIONS — 1937, 1954, 1976, AND 2018, EACH WITH A STYLE OF ITS OWN

A FILM FESTIVAL WINNER

MOVIE TITLE: _____

YEAR RELEASED: _____

ASPECT RATIO: _____ RUN TIME: _____

GENRE: _____ RATED: _____

STARRING: _____

_____

DATE CHALLENGE COMPLETED:

_____

MY RATING:

☆☆☆☆☆

DIRECTED BY: _____

PRODUCED BY: _____

WRITTEN BY: _____

MUSIC BY: _____

AWARDS RECEIVED: _____

_____

WHY DID YOU CHOOSE THIS PARTICULAR FILM? _____

_____

HAVE YOU SEEN THIS MOVIE BEFORE? _____

WOULD YOU RECOMMEND THIS FILM? WHY OR WHY NOT? _____

_____

_____

_____

WHICH CHARACTER WERE YOU MOST ABLE TO IDENTIFY WITH OR CONNECT WITH?
IN WHAT WAY? _____
_____
_____

BEST LINE OR MEMORABLE QUOTE: _____
_____
_____

WERE YOU SUPRISED BY THE ENDING? WHAT WOULD YOU DO DIFFERENTLY? ____
_____
_____
_____

WHICH FILM FESTIVAL AWARD DID THIS FILM RECEIVE? _____
WHAT DID YOU LIKE ABOUT THE FILM? _____
_____
_____

IS THERE ANYTHING YOU WOULD HAVE DONE DIFFERENTLY? _____
_____
_____
_____

ANYTHING ELSE YOU'D LIKE TO ADD? _____
_____

BEFORE ITS 1999 SUNDANCE PREMIERE, 19 HOURS OF FOOTAGE FOR "THE
BLAIR WITCH PROJECT" WENT THROUGH EIGHT MONTHS OF EDITING

CHOOSE A
BLACK & WHITE FILM

MOVIE TITLE: _____

YEAR RELEASED: _____

ASPECT RATIO: _____ RUN TIME: _____

GENRE: _____ RATED: _____

STARRING: _____

_____

DATE CHALLENGE COMPLETED:

_____

MY RATING:

☆ ☆ ☆ ☆ ☆

DIRECTED BY: _____

PRODUCED BY: _____

WRITTEN BY: _____

MUSIC BY: _____

AWARDS RECEIVED: _____

_____

WHY DID YOU CHOOSE THIS PARTICULAR FILM? _____

_____

HAVE YOU SEEN THIS MOVIE BEFORE? _____

WOULD YOU RECOMMEND THIS FILM? WHY OR WHY NOT? _____

_____

_____

_____

WHICH CHARACTER WERE YOU MOST ABLE TO IDENTIFY WITH OR CONNECT WITH? IN WHAT WAY? _____

_____

_____

BEST LINE OR MEMORABLE QUOTE: _____

_____

_____

WERE YOU SUPRISED BY THE ENDING? WHAT WOULD YOU DO DIFFERENTLY? ____

_____

_____

_____

DO YOU FEEL THIS FILM WOULD BE BETTER OR WORSE IF IT WERE IN COLOR? WHY DO YOU FEEL THAT WAY? _____

_____

_____

_____

_____

_____

ANYTHING ELSE YOU'D LIKE TO ADD? _____

_____

 IN "SCHINDLER'S LIST" (1993), THE LITTLE GIRL IN THE RED COAT WAS
FILM FACT BASED ON A REAL PERSON, A KRAKOW GHETTO SURVIVOR.

A SEQUEL

MOVIE TITLE: _____

YEAR RELEASED: _____

ASPECT RATIO: _____ RUN TIME: _____

GENRE: _____ RATED: _____

STARRING: _____

_____

DATE CHALLENGE COMPLETED:

_____

MY RATING:

☆ ☆ ☆ ☆ ☆

DIRECTED BY: _____

PRODUCED BY: _____

WRITTEN BY: _____

MUSIC BY: _____

AWARDS RECEIVED: _____

_____

WHY DID YOU CHOOSE THIS PARTICULAR FILM? _____

_____

HAVE YOU SEEN THIS MOVIE BEFORE? _____

WOULD YOU RECOMMEND THIS FILM? WHY OR WHY NOT? _____

_____

_____

_____

WHICH CHARACTER WERE YOU MOST ABLE TO IDENTIFY WITH OR CONNECT WITH? IN WHAT WAY? _____

_____

_____

BEST LINE OR MEMORABLE QUOTE: _____

_____

_____

WERE YOU SUPRISED BY THE ENDING? WHAT WOULD YOU DO DIFFERENTLY? _____

_____

_____

_____

WAS THIS SEQUEL BETTER OR WORSE THAN ITS PREDECESSOR? WHY? _____

_____

_____

_____

_____

DID THIS FILM MEET YOUR EXPECTATIONS? WHY OR WHY NOT? _____

_____

_____

ANYTHING ELSE YOU'D LIKE TO ADD? _____

_____

FILM FACT "STAR TREK: THE WRATH OF KHAN" (1982) WAS THE FIRST TIME A MOVIE WAS MADE AS A SEQUEL TO A SPECIFIC TELEVISION SHOW EPISODE

SET DURING THE
GREAT DEPRESSION

MOVIE TITLE: _____

YEAR RELEASED: _____

ASPECT RATIO: _____ RUN TIME: _____

GENRE: _____ RATED: _____

STARRING: _____

_____

DIRECTED BY: _____

PRODUCED BY: _____

WRITTEN BY: _____

MUSIC BY: _____

AWARDS RECEIVED: _____

_____

DATE CHALLENGE COMPLETED:

_____

MY RATING:

☆☆☆☆☆

WHY DID YOU CHOOSE THIS PARTICULAR FILM? _____

_____

HAVE YOU SEEN THIS MOVIE BEFORE? _____

WOULD YOU RECOMMEND THIS FILM? WHY OR WHY NOT? _____

_____

_____

_____

WHICH CHARACTER WERE YOU MOST ABLE TO IDENTIFY WITH OR CONNECT WITH?
IN WHAT WAY? _____
_____
_____

BEST LINE OR MEMORABLE QUOTE: _____
_____
_____

WERE YOU SUPRISED BY THE ENDING? WHAT WOULD YOU DO DIFFERENTLY? _____
_____
_____
_____

IMAGINE YOURSELF IN THIS TIME PERIOD. WHAT WOULD YOU DO IF YOU WERE IN
THE SAME POSITION AS THE MAIN CHARACTER? _____
_____
_____
_____
_____
_____
_____

ANYTHING ELSE YOU'D LIKE TO ADD? _____
_____

FILM FACT AROUND 8000 GIRLS AUDITIONED FOR THE LEAD ROLE IN "ANNIE"
(1982) BY TAKING TURNS SINGING A PART OF "TOMORROW"

A BOOK ADAPTATION

MOVIE TITLE: _____

YEAR RELEASED: _____

ASPECT RATIO: _____ RUN TIME: _____

GENRE: _____ RATED: _____

STARRING: _____

_____

DATE CHALLENGE COMPLETED:

_____

MY RATING:

☆ ☆ ☆ ☆ ☆

DIRECTED BY: _____

PRODUCED BY: _____

WRITTEN BY: _____

MUSIC BY: _____

AWARDS RECEIVED: _____

_____

WHY DID YOU CHOOSE THIS PARTICULAR FILM? _____

_____

HAVE YOU SEEN THIS MOVIE BEFORE? _____

WOULD YOU RECOMMEND THIS FILM? WHY OR WHY NOT? _____

_____

_____

_____

WHICH CHARACTER WERE YOU MOST ABLE TO IDENTIFY WITH OR CONNECT WITH?
IN WHAT WAY? _____

_____

_____

BEST LINE OR MEMORABLE QUOTE: _____

_____

_____

WERE YOU SUPRISED BY THE ENDING? WHAT WOULD YOU DO DIFFERENTLY? _____

_____

_____

_____

HAVE YOU READ THE BOOK? CONSIDERING THE TIME RESTRICTIONS A MOVIE HAS,
DID THE FILM CAPTURE THE ORIGINAL STORY WELL? _____

_____

_____

_____

_____

_____

ANYTHING ELSE YOU'D LIKE TO ADD? _____

_____

MOVIES THAT ARE ADAPTED FROM BOOKS HISTORICALLY HAVE A
HIGHER PROBABILITY OF BECOMING A BOX-OFFICE HIT.

YOUR FAVORITE FILM

MOVIE TITLE: _____

YEAR RELEASED: _____

ASPECT RATIO: _____ RUN TIME: _____

GENRE: _____ RATED: _____

STARRING: _____

_____

DIRECTED BY: _____

PRODUCED BY: _____

WRITTEN BY: _____

MUSIC BY: _____

AWARDS RECEIVED: _____

_____

DATE CHALLENGE COMPLETED:

_____

MY RATING:

☆ ☆ ☆ ☆ ☆

HOW MANY TIMES HAVE YOU SEEN THIS MOVIE (APPROXIMATELY)? _____

WHAT MAKES THIS ONE YOUR FAVORITE? _____

_____

_____

_____

_____

_____

WHO IS YOUR FAVORITE CHARACTER? WHY?_____

_____

_____

WHICH CHARACTER ARE YOU MOST ABLE TO IDENTIFY WITH OR CONNECT WITH?
IN WHAT WAY?_____

_____

_____

BEST LINE OR MEMORABLE QUOTE:_____

_____

_____

FAVORITE SCENE:_____

_____

_____

_____

DO YOU HAVE AN INTERESTING TIDBIT ABOUT YOU AND THIS MOVIE?_____

_____

_____

_____

_____

ANYTHING ELSE YOU'D LIKE TO ADD?_____

_____

BETWEEN MOVIE THEATERS, STREAMING & HOME VIDEO, THE AVERAGE
FILM FACT AMERICAN WILL WATCH ABOUT 5000 FILMS IN THEIR LIFETIME

A NATURAL DISASTER FILM

MOVIE TITLE: _____

YEAR RELEASED: _____

ASPECT RATIO: _____ RUN TIME: _____

GENRE: _____ RATED: _____

STARRING: _____

_____

DIRECTED BY: _____

PRODUCED BY: _____

WRITTEN BY: _____

MUSIC BY: _____

AWARDS RECEIVED: _____

_____

DATE CHALLENGE COMPLETED:

_____

MY RATING:

☆ ☆ ☆ ☆ ☆

WHY DID YOU CHOOSE THIS PARTICULAR FILM? _____

_____

HAVE YOU SEEN THIS MOVIE BEFORE? _____

WOULD YOU RECOMMEND THIS FILM? WHY OR WHY NOT? _____

_____

_____

_____

WHICH CHARACTER WERE YOU MOST ABLE TO IDENTIFY WITH OR CONNECT WITH?
IN WHAT WAY? _____

_____

_____

BEST LINE OR MEMORABLE QUOTE: _____

_____

_____

WERE YOU SUPRISED BY THE ENDING? WHAT WOULD YOU DO DIFFERENTLY? _____

_____

_____

WHAT ARE SOME THINGS YOU WOULD DO IF YOU FACED A SIMILAR DISASTER? _____

_____

_____

_____

_____

_____

_____

ANYTHING ELSE YOU'D LIKE TO ADD? _____

_____

FILM FACT A 707 BOEING JET WAS USED ON THE SET OF "TWISTER" (1996) TO HELP GENERATE THE 200 MPH WIND SPEEDS PRODUCED BY THE TORNADOES.

SET IN YOUR
LOCATION OR REGION

MOVIE TITLE: _____

YEAR RELEASED: _____

ASPECT RATIO: _____ RUN TIME: _____

GENRE: _____ RATED: _____

STARRING: _____

_____

DIRECTED BY: _____

PRODUCED BY: _____

WRITTEN BY: _____

MUSIC BY: _____

AWARDS RECEIVED: _____

_____

DATE CHALLENGE COMPLETED:

_____

MY RATING:

☆ ☆ ☆ ☆ ☆

WHY DID YOU CHOOSE THIS PARTICULAR FILM? _____

_____

HAVE YOU SEEN THIS MOVIE BEFORE? _____

WOULD YOU RECOMMEND THIS FILM? WHY OR WHY NOT? _____

_____

_____

_____

WHICH CHARACTER WERE YOU MOST ABLE TO IDENTIFY WITH OR CONNECT WITH?
IN WHAT WAY? _____
_____
_____

BEST LINE OR MEMORABLE QUOTE: _____
_____
_____

WERE YOU SUPRISED BY THE ENDING? WHAT WOULD YOU DO DIFFERENTLY? _____
_____
_____
_____

HOW WELL DO YOU FEEL THE FILM PORTRAYED YOUR REGION? WHAT SUBTLE
DETAILS WERE THERE THAT "COMPLETED" THE PICTURE? _____
_____
_____
_____
_____
_____

ANYTHING ELSE YOU'D LIKE TO ADD? _____
_____

ONE-EYED WILLY'S SHIP IN "THE GOONIES" (1985) WAS SUPPOSED TO
RESEMBLE ERROL FLYNN'S SHIP FROM THE MOVIE "THE SEA HAWK."

ABOUT AN ACTUAL
COMPOSER, MUSICIAN, BAND OR GROUP

MOVIE TITLE: _____

YEAR RELEASED: _____

ASPECT RATIO: _____ RUN TIME: _____

GENRE: _____ RATED: _____

STARRING: _____

_____

DATE CHALLENGE COMPLETED:

_____

MY RATING:

☆ ☆ ☆ ☆ ☆

DIRECTED BY: _____

PRODUCED BY: _____

WRITTEN BY: _____

MUSIC BY: _____

AWARDS RECEIVED: _____

_____

WHY DID YOU CHOOSE THIS PARTICULAR FILM? _____

_____

HAVE YOU SEEN THIS MOVIE BEFORE? _____

WOULD YOU RECOMMEND THIS FILM? WHY OR WHY NOT? _____

_____

_____

_____

WHICH CHARACTER WERE YOU MOST ABLE TO IDENTIFY WITH OR CONNECT WITH?
IN WHAT WAY? _____

_____

_____

BEST LINE OR MEMORABLE QUOTE: _____

_____

_____

WERE YOU SUPRISED BY THE ENDING? WHAT WOULD YOU DO DIFFERENTLY? _____

_____

_____

_____

IS THE COMPOSER/MUSICIAN/BAND/GROUP FEATURED IN THE FILM ONE THAT YOU
REGULARLY LISTEN TO? _____

_____

_____

WHAT NEW INFORMATION DID YOU LEARN? _____

_____

_____

_____

ANYTHING ELSE YOU'D LIKE TO ADD? _____

_____

A FOREIGN FILM

MOVIE TITLE: _____

YEAR RELEASED: _____

ASPECT RATIO: _____ RUN TIME: _____

GENRE: _____ RATED: _____

STARRING: _____

_____

DIRECTED BY: _____

PRODUCED BY: _____

WRITTEN BY: _____

MUSIC BY: _____

AWARDS RECEIVED: _____

_____

DATE CHALLENGE COMPLETED:

_____

MY RATING:

☆ ☆ ☆ ☆ ☆

WHY DID YOU CHOOSE THIS PARTICULAR FILM? _____

_____

HAVE YOU SEEN THIS MOVIE BEFORE? _____

WOULD YOU RECOMMEND THIS FILM? WHY OR WHY NOT? _____

_____

_____

_____

WHICH CHARACTER WERE YOU MOST ABLE TO IDENTIFY WITH OR CONNECT WITH?
IN WHAT WAY? _____
_____
_____

BEST LINE OR MEMORABLE QUOTE: _____
_____
_____

WERE YOU SUPRISED BY THE ENDING? WHAT WOULD YOU DO DIFFERENTLY?_____
_____
_____
_____

WHERE WAS THIS MOVIE FILMED?_____
WAS THE FILM DUBBED OR SUBTITLED?_____
DID YOU NOTICE ANY CULTURAL DIFFERENCES BETWEEN THIS FOREIGN FILM AND
RECENTLY WATCHED DOMESTIC FILMS IN THE SAME GENRE OR TIME PERIOD?_____
_____
_____
_____
_____

ANYTHING ELSE YOU'D LIKE TO ADD? _____
_____

FILM FACT "MAD MAX" (1979) WAS FILMED IN THE MELBOURNE, AUSTRALIA AREA FOR
AROUND $350K (LESS THAN MOST MOVIE'S ADVERTISING BUDGETS)

A HOLIDAY MOVIE

MOVIE TITLE: _____

YEAR RELEASED: _____

ASPECT RATIO: _____ RUN TIME: _____

GENRE: _____ RATED: _____

STARRING: _____

_____

DATE CHALLENGE COMPLETED:

_____

MY RATING:

☆ ☆ ☆ ☆ ☆

DIRECTED BY: _____

PRODUCED BY: _____

WRITTEN BY: _____

MUSIC BY: _____

AWARDS RECEIVED: _____

_____

WHY DID YOU CHOOSE THIS PARTICULAR FILM? _____

_____

HAVE YOU SEEN THIS MOVIE BEFORE? _____

WOULD YOU RECOMMEND THIS FILM? WHY OR WHY NOT? _____

_____

_____

_____

WHICH CHARACTER WERE YOU MOST ABLE TO IDENTIFY WITH OR CONNECT WITH?
IN WHAT WAY? _____

_____

_____

BEST LINE OR MEMORABLE QUOTE: _____

_____

_____

WERE YOU SUPRISED BY THE ENDING? WHAT WOULD YOU DO DIFFERENTLY? ____

_____

_____

_____

DO YOU CELEBRATE THE HOLIDAY FEATURED IN THIS FILM? _____

IF SO, HOW ARE YOUR OWN CELEBRATIONS SIMILAR TO OR DIFFERENT FROM

THOSE PORTRAYED IN THE FILM? _____

_____

_____

_____

_____

ANYTHING ELSE YOU'D LIKE TO ADD? _____

_____

FILM FACT THE THANKSGIVING DAY PARADE IN "MIRACLE ON 34TH STREET" (1947)
WAS THE ACTUAL 1946 PARADE WITH EDMUND GWENN AS SANTA

THE FIRST FILM
OF A FAMOUS DIRECTOR

MOVIE TITLE: _____

YEAR RELEASED: _____

ASPECT RATIO: _____ RUN TIME: _____

GENRE: _____ RATED: _____

STARRING: _____

_____

DIRECTED BY: _____

PRODUCED BY: _____

WRITTEN BY: _____

MUSIC BY: _____

AWARDS RECEIVED: _____

_____

DATE CHALLENGE COMPLETED:
_____
MY RATING:
☆ ☆ ☆ ☆ ☆

WHY DID YOU CHOOSE THIS PARTICULAR FILM? _____

_____

HAVE YOU SEEN THIS MOVIE BEFORE? _____

WOULD YOU RECOMMEND THIS FILM? WHY OR WHY NOT? _____

_____

_____

_____

WHICH CHARACTER WERE YOU MOST ABLE TO IDENTIFY WITH OR CONNECT WITH?
IN WHAT WAY? _____
_____
_____

BEST LINE OR MEMORABLE QUOTE:_____
_____
_____

WERE YOU SUPRISED BY THE ENDING? WHAT WOULD YOU DO DIFFERENTLY? _____
_____
_____
_____

WHAT IS YOUR OVERALL OPINION OF THIS DIRECTOR'S FIRST FILM?_____
_____
_____
_____

CAN YOU SEE HINTS OF THEIR LATER STYLE IN THIS ONE?_____
_____
_____
_____

IS THERE ANYTHING ELSE YOU WANT TO MENTION ABOUT THIS MOVIE?_____
_____

FILM FACT "...MY FIRST BRUTAL EXPERIENCE OF FILMMAKING – CALL IT A BAPTISM
BY FIRE..." – OLIVER STONE IN 2014 REFERRING TO "SEIZURE" (1974)

SET IN A COLLEGE

MOVIE TITLE: _____

YEAR RELEASED: _____

ASPECT RATIO: _____ RUN TIME: _____

GENRE: _____ RATED: _____

STARRING: _____
_____

DIRECTED BY: _____

PRODUCED BY: _____

WRITTEN BY: _____

MUSIC BY: _____

AWARDS RECEIVED: _____
_____

WHY DID YOU CHOOSE THIS PARTICULAR FILM? _____
_____

HAVE YOU SEEN THIS MOVIE BEFORE? _____

WOULD YOU RECOMMEND THIS FILM? WHY OR WHY NOT? _____
_____
_____
_____

DATE CHALLENGE COMPLETED:

_____

MY RATING:

☆ ☆ ☆ ☆ ☆

WHICH CHARACTER WERE YOU MOST ABLE TO IDENTIFY WITH OR CONNECT WITH? IN WHAT WAY? _____

_____

_____

BEST LINE OR MEMORABLE QUOTE: _____

_____

_____

IF YOU ATTENDED COLLEGE, DID THIS FILM RESEMBLE YOUR COLLEGE LIFE? IF SO, HOW? _____

_____

_____

_____

_____

WOULD YOU ATTEND THIS COLLEGE? WHY OR WHY NOT? _____

_____

_____

_____

ANYTHING ELSE YOU'D LIKE TO ADD? _____

_____

_____

THREE DIFFERENT COLLEGES WERE USED TO CREATE GRAND LAKES UNIVERSITY IN "BACK TO SCHOOL" (1986)

A FILM THAT HAS WON
BEST MUSIC (ORIGINAL SCORE)

MOVIE TITLE: _____

YEAR RELEASED: _____

ASPECT RATIO: _____ RUN TIME: _____

GENRE: _____ RATED: _____

STARRING: _____

_____

DATE CHALLENGE COMPLETED:

_____

MY RATING:

☆ ☆ ☆ ☆ ☆

DIRECTED BY: _____

PRODUCED BY: _____

WRITTEN BY: _____

MUSIC BY: _____

AWARDS RECEIVED: _____

_____

WHY DID YOU CHOOSE THIS PARTICULAR FILM? _____

_____

HAVE YOU SEEN THIS MOVIE BEFORE? _____

WOULD YOU RECOMMEND THIS FILM? WHY OR WHY NOT? _____

_____

_____

_____

WHICH CHARACTER WERE YOU MOST ABLE TO IDENTIFY WITH OR CONNECT WITH? IN WHAT WAY? _____

_____

_____

BEST LINE OR MEMORABLE QUOTE: _____

_____

_____

WERE YOU SUPRISED BY THE ENDING? WHAT WOULD YOU DO DIFFERENTLY? _____

_____

_____

_____

DO YOU FEEL THE MUSIC SCORE CARRIED THE FILM, OR ENHANCED IT? EXPLAIN.

_____

_____

_____

_____

IS THE SOUNDTRACK ONE YOU WOULD BE HAPPY TO LISTEN TO WITHOUT THE MOVIE? _____

_____

ANYTHING ELSE YOU'D LIKE TO ADD? _____

_____

A FILM THAT HAS BEEN
ADAPTED FROM A PLAY

MOVIE TITLE: _____

YEAR RELEASED: _____

ASPECT RATIO: _____ RUN TIME: _____

GENRE: _____ RATED: _____

STARRING: _____

_____

DATE CHALLENGE COMPLETED:

_____

MY RATING:

☆ ☆ ☆ ☆ ☆

DIRECTED BY: _____

PRODUCED BY: _____

WRITTEN BY: _____

MUSIC BY: _____

AWARDS RECEIVED: _____

_____

WHY DID YOU CHOOSE THIS PARTICULAR FILM? _____

_____

HAVE YOU SEEN THIS MOVIE BEFORE? _____

WOULD YOU RECOMMEND THIS FILM? WHY OR WHY NOT? _____

_____

_____

_____

WHICH CHARACTER WERE YOU MOST ABLE TO IDENTIFY WITH OR CONNECT WITH?
IN WHAT WAY? _____

_____

_____

BEST LINE OR MEMORABLE QUOTE: _____

_____

_____

WERE YOU SUPRISED BY THE ENDING? WHAT WOULD YOU DO DIFFERENTLY? ____

_____

_____

_____

HAVE YOU SEEN THE PLAY BEFORE? IF SO, HOW SIMILAR IS THIS FILM VERSION?
IF YOU HAVE NOT SEEN THE PLAY, DID THIS FILM MAKE YOU WANT TO? _____

_____

_____

_____

_____

_____

ANYTHING ELSE YOU'D LIKE TO ADD? _____

_____

 "STEEL MAGNOLIAS" (1989) IS AN ADAPTATION OF A PLAY BY THE SAME
FILM FACT NAME. THE PLAY HAD NO ON-STAGE ROLES FOR MEN.

A FILM WITH YOUR FAVORITE ACTOR OR ACTRESS

MOVIE TITLE: _____

YEAR RELEASED: _____

ASPECT RATIO: _____ RUN TIME: _____

GENRE: _____ RATED: _____

STARRING: _____

_____

DATE CHALLENGE COMPLETED:

_____

MY RATING:

☆ ☆ ☆ ☆ ☆

DIRECTED BY: _____

PRODUCED BY: _____

WRITTEN BY: _____

MUSIC BY: _____

AWARDS RECEIVED: _____

_____

WHY DID YOU CHOOSE THIS PARTICULAR FILM? _____

_____

HAVE YOU SEEN THIS MOVIE BEFORE? _____

WOULD YOU RECOMMEND THIS FILM? WHY OR WHY NOT? _____

_____

_____

_____

_____

WHICH CHARACTER WERE YOU MOST ABLE TO IDENTIFY WITH OR CONNECT WITH?
IN WHAT WAY? _____

_____

_____

BEST LINE OR MEMORABLE QUOTE: _____

_____

_____

WERE YOU SUPRISED BY THE ENDING? WHAT WOULD YOU DO DIFFERENTLY? ____

_____

_____

WOULD YOU LIKE TO SEE THIS STAR CHALLENGE THEMSELVES WITH A DIFFERENT
GENRE? WHAT GENRE DO YOU FEEL THEY COULD DO WELL IN? _____

_____

_____

_____

_____

_____

ANYTHING ELSE YOU'D LIKE TO ADD? _____

_____

WITH DESIGNER LOANS AND OVER $1 MILLION SPENT ON COSTUMING, "THE
DEVIL WEARS PRADA" (2006) MADE QUITE A FASHION STATEMENT.

ABOUT A
FAMOUS PERSON

MOVIE TITLE: _____

YEAR RELEASED: _____

ASPECT RATIO: _____ RUN TIME: _____

GENRE: _____ RATED: _____

STARRING: _____

_____

DATE CHALLENGE COMPLETED:

_____

MY RATING:

☆ ☆ ☆ ☆ ☆

DIRECTED BY: _____

PRODUCED BY: _____

WRITTEN BY: _____

MUSIC BY: _____

AWARDS RECEIVED: _____

_____

WHY DID YOU CHOOSE THIS PARTICULAR FILM? _____

_____

HAVE YOU SEEN THIS MOVIE BEFORE? _____

WOULD YOU RECOMMEND THIS FILM? WHY OR WHY NOT? _____

_____

_____

_____

WHICH CHARACTER WERE YOU MOST ABLE TO IDENTIFY WITH OR CONNECT WITH?
IN WHAT WAY? _____

_____

_____

BEST LINE OR MEMORABLE QUOTE: _____

_____

_____

WERE YOU SUPRISED BY THE ENDING? WHAT WOULD YOU DO DIFFERENTLY? _____

_____

_____

_____

WHAT IS SOMETHING NEW YOU LEARNED ABOUT THIS PERSON? _____

_____

_____

_____

_____

DID THIS FILM CHANGE YOUR VIEW OF THIS PERSON? IF SO, HOW? _____

_____

_____

_____

_____

FILM FACT SEVENTY-NINE SETS WERE CONSTRUCTED FOR "CLEOPATRA" (1963) AND
26,000 COSTUMES WERE CREATED INCLUDING 65 FOR LIZ TAYLOR

SET IN A COUNTRY
YOU WANT TO VISIT

MOVIE TITLE: _____

YEAR RELEASED: _____

ASPECT RATIO: _____ RUN TIME: _____

GENRE: _____ RATED: _____

STARRING: _____

_____

DATE CHALLENGE COMPLETED:

_____

MY RATING:

☆ ☆ ☆ ☆ ☆

DIRECTED BY: _____

PRODUCED BY: _____

WRITTEN BY: _____

MUSIC BY: _____

AWARDS RECEIVED: _____

_____

WHY DID YOU CHOOSE THIS PARTICULAR FILM? _____

_____

HAVE YOU SEEN THIS MOVIE BEFORE? _____

WOULD YOU RECOMMEND THIS FILM? WHY OR WHY NOT? _____

_____

_____

_____

WHICH CHARACTER WERE YOU MOST ABLE TO IDENTIFY WITH OR CONNECT WITH? IN WHAT WAY? _____

_____

_____

BEST LINE OR MEMORABLE QUOTE: _____

_____

_____

WERE YOU SUPRISED BY THE ENDING? WHAT WOULD YOU DO DIFFERENTLY? _____

_____

_____

_____

HOW FAMILIAR ARE YOU WITH THE COUNTRY THE FILM WAS SET IN? DO YOU FEEL THE FILM REALISTICALLY PORTRAYED LIFE IN THIS COUNTRY? _____

_____

_____

_____

_____

_____

ANYTHING ELSE YOU'D LIKE TO ADD? _____

_____

THE GOLDEN HINDE, A REPLICA OF A 1570'S GALLEON, WAS USED FOR BOTH THE ERASMUS AND THE BLACK SHIP IN "SHOGUN" (1980)

A FILM
BASED AROUND A RELIGION

MOVIE TITLE: _____

YEAR RELEASED: _____

ASPECT RATIO: _____ RUN TIME: _____

GENRE: _____ RATED: _____

STARRING: _____

_____

DATE CHALLENGE COMPLETED:

_____

MY RATING:

☆ ☆ ☆ ☆ ☆

DIRECTED BY: _____

PRODUCED BY: _____

WRITTEN BY: _____

MUSIC BY: _____

AWARDS RECEIVED: _____

_____

WHY DID YOU CHOOSE THIS PARTICULAR FILM? _____

_____

HAVE YOU SEEN THIS MOVIE BEFORE? _____

WOULD YOU RECOMMEND THIS FILM? WHY OR WHY NOT? _____

_____

_____

_____

WHICH CHARACTER WERE YOU MOST ABLE TO IDENTIFY WITH OR CONNECT WITH?
IN WHAT WAY? _____

_____

_____

BEST LINE OR MEMORABLE QUOTE: _____

_____

_____

WERE YOU SUPRISED BY THE ENDING? WHAT WOULD YOU DO DIFFERENTLY? _____

_____

_____

_____

WHAT IS THE RELIGION FEATURED? HOW FAMILIAR ARE YOU WITH THIS RELIGION?

_____

_____

WAS THE RELIGION REPRESENTED WELL OR DO YOU FEEL IT WAS EMBELLISHED
TO CREATE A MORE ENTERTAINING STORY? EXPLAIN. _____

_____

_____

_____

ANYTHING ELSE YOU'D LIKE TO ADD? _____

_____

FILM FACT   THE CHARIOT RACE IN "BEN-HUR" (1959) TOOK A YEAR OF PREP-
ARATION AND 5 WEEKS (SPREAD OVER 3 MONTHS) TO FILM.

A FILM CELEBRATING ITS 50TH ANNIVERSARY THIS YEAR

MOVIE TITLE: _____

YEAR RELEASED: _____

ASPECT RATIO: _____ RUN TIME: _____

GENRE: _____ RATED: _____

STARRING: _____

_____

DATE CHALLENGE COMPLETED:

_____

MY RATING:

☆ ☆ ☆ ☆ ☆

DIRECTED BY: _____

PRODUCED BY: _____

WRITTEN BY: _____

MUSIC BY: _____

AWARDS RECEIVED: _____

_____

WHY DID YOU CHOOSE THIS PARTICULAR FILM? _____

_____

HAVE YOU SEEN THIS MOVIE BEFORE? _____

WOULD YOU RECOMMEND THIS FILM? WHY OR WHY NOT? _____

_____

_____

_____

WHICH CHARACTER WERE YOU MOST ABLE TO IDENTIFY WITH OR CONNECT WITH?
IN WHAT WAY? _____
_____
_____

BEST LINE OR MEMORABLE QUOTE: _____
_____
_____

WERE YOU SUPRISED BY THE ENDING? WHAT WOULD YOU DO DIFFERENTLY? ____
_____
_____
_____

DO YOU FEEL THIS FILM HAS AS MUCH "IMPACT" NOW AS IT DID WHEN IT WAS
RELEASED 50 YEARS AGO? EXPLAIN. _____
_____
_____
_____
_____
_____

ANYTHING ELSE YOU'D LIKE TO ADD? _____
_____

 IN 2019, "EASY RIDER", "HELLO, DOLLY!" AND "A BOY CALLED
FILM FACT CHARLIE BROWN" ALL CELEBRATED THEIR 50TH ANNIVERSARIES

A FILM YOU
PERSONALLY RELATE TO

MOVIE TITLE: _____

YEAR RELEASED: _____

ASPECT RATIO: _____ RUN TIME: _____

GENRE: _____ RATED: _____

STARRING: _____

_____

DATE CHALLENGE COMPLETED:

_____

MY RATING:

☆ ☆ ☆ ☆ ☆

DIRECTED BY: _____

PRODUCED BY: _____

WRITTEN BY: _____

MUSIC BY: _____

AWARDS RECEIVED: _____

_____

WHY DID YOU CHOOSE THIS PARTICULAR FILM OVER OTHERS? _____

_____

HAVE YOU SEEN THIS MOVIE BEFORE? _____

WOULD YOU RECOMMEND THIS FILM? WHY OR WHY NOT? _____

_____

_____

_____

WHICH CHARACTER WERE YOU MOST ABLE TO IDENTIFY WITH OR CONNECT WITH?
IN WHAT WAY? _____

_____

_____

BEST LINE OR MEMORABLE QUOTE: _____

_____

_____

TELL HOW YOU PERSONALLY RELATE TO THIS FILM. _____

_____

_____

_____

_____

_____

_____

WHAT EMOTIONS DID YOU EXPERIENCE WATCHING THIS FILM? _____

_____

_____

_____

ANYTHING ELSE YOU'D LIKE TO ADD? _____

_____

WHY ALL THE REFERENCES TO SPAM® IN "50 FIRST DATES" (2004)?
FILM FACT 7 MILLION SPAM® PRODUCTS ARE EATEN IN HAWAII EVERY YEAR.

A MOVIE RELEASED
THE DECADE YOU WERE BORN

MOVIE TITLE: _____

YEAR RELEASED: _____

ASPECT RATIO: _____ RUN TIME: _____

GENRE: _____ RATED: _____

STARRING: _____

_____

DIRECTED BY: _____

PRODUCED BY: _____

WRITTEN BY: _____

MUSIC BY: _____

AWARDS RECEIVED: _____

_____

DATE CHALLENGE COMPLETED:

_____

MY RATING:

☆ ☆ ☆ ☆ ☆

WHY DID YOU CHOOSE THIS PARTICULAR FILM? _____

_____

HAVE YOU SEEN THIS MOVIE BEFORE? _____

WOULD YOU RECOMMEND THIS FILM? WHY OR WHY NOT? _____

_____

_____

_____

WHICH CHARACTER WERE YOU MOST ABLE TO IDENTIFY WITH OR CONNECT WITH? IN WHAT WAY? _____

_____

_____

BEST LINE OR MEMORABLE QUOTE: _____

_____

_____

WERE YOU SUPRISED BY THE ENDING? WHAT WOULD YOU DO DIFFERENTLY? ____

_____

_____

_____

HOW HAVE MOVIES CHANGED SINCE THIS WAS RELEASED? _____

_____

_____

IMAGINE THIS MOVIE BEING REMADE TODAY. WOULD THE STORY NEED TO BE CHANGED? WHO WOULD YOU WANT TO PLAY THE MAIN CHARACTERS? _____

_____

_____

_____

ANYTHING ELSE YOU'D LIKE TO ADD? _____

_____

POPCORN WAS SOLD BY STREET VENDORS OUTSIDE MOVIE THEATERS
FILM FACT UNTIL THEATER OWNERS DECIDED TO CUT OUT THE MIDDLE MAN

THAT'S A WRAP!